THE REMOTE WORK: STRATEGIES FOR SUCCESSFUL FREELANCING

First edition. September 25, 2024.

Copyright © 2024 Yash d..

ISBN: 979-8227325464

Written by Yash d..

Table of Contents

The Remote Work: Strategies for Successful Freelancing

Author: Yash D.

Summary

In "The Remote Work: Strategies for Successful Freelancing," the author delves into the evolving landscape of remote work and its implications for freelancers. The book begins by addressing the fundamental shift in work dynamics brought about by technology and globalization, highlighting how these changes have opened up new opportunities for independent workers. It emphasizes the importance of adaptability and staying current with industry trends to thrive in a competitive freelance market.

The author outlines practical strategies for building a successful freelance career, focusing on essential skills such as time management, effective communication, and self-discipline. By providing actionable tips and tools, the book guides freelancers in establishing a productive workspace, setting clear goals, and maintaining a healthy work-life balance. Additionally, it explores the significance of networking and branding, offering insights on how freelancers can effectively market themselves and attract clients.

Furthermore, the book addresses common challenges faced by remote workers, including isolation and distractions, and presents strategies for overcoming these obstacles. It encourages readers to cultivate a growth mindset and continuously seek opportunities for professional development. In conclusion, "The Remote Work: Strategies for Successful Freelancing" serves as a comprehensive guide for anyone looking to navigate the freelance landscape with confidence and achieve long-term success.

Chapter 1

Introduction to Remote Work

1.1 What is Remote Work?

Remote work refers to a professional environment where employees work outside of a traditional office setting. It is often called "telecommuting," "telework," or "working from home." Remote workers use digital communication tools such as email, video conferencing, and collaboration software to stay connected with colleagues and complete their tasks.

Instead of being physically present at a company's headquarters or office space, remote employees work from various locations, whether from home, a coffee shop, a coworking space, or even while traveling. Remote work allows for greater flexibility in terms of where and when work gets done, as long as the work is completed efficiently and meets the company's expectations.

1.2 History of Remote Work

Remote work isn't a new concept. Even before the internet, some people worked remotely. For example, freelance writers, consultants, and salespeople have worked outside of traditional office environments for decades.

However, the widespread adoption of remote work gained momentum with the advancement of technology, particularly in the late 20th and early 21st centuries. The internet, email, and cloud computing revolutionized how people collaborate, making remote work more feasible.

For instance, in the 1990s, companies like IBM experimented with allowing employees to work from home, and it paved the way for remote work models that companies of all sizes would later adopt.

The COVID-19 pandemic in 2020 accelerated the growth of remote work, with many companies adopting remote or hybrid work models as a necessity to maintain operations while keeping employees safe. Even post-pandemic, many organizations and workers realized the benefits of remote work, making it a lasting trend.

1.3 Benefits of Remote Work

Remote work has numerous benefits, not only for employees but also for employers. Let's look at some of the key advantages:

1. Flexibility: One of the most significant advantages of remote work is the flexibility it provides. Employees can structure their day in a way that suits their personal preferences, balancing work and life responsibilities. For example, a parent may choose to work early in the morning and late in the evening, allowing them to spend quality time with their children during the day.

2. Increased Productivity: Many studies suggest that remote workers can be more productive than their office-based counterparts. Without the distractions of office environments (like impromptu meetings, office gossip, or long commute times), employees can focus more on their work. For instance, someone who would usually spend an hour commuting to work can now use that time to complete tasks or start the day more energized.

3. Cost Savings: Both employees and employers can save money through remote work. Employees save on commuting costs, buying lunch, and work attire. Employers save on overhead costs such as rent, utilities, and office supplies. For example, companies like Buffer operate remotely and report significant savings on office space.

4. Access to a Global Talent Pool: With remote work, companies are no longer restricted to hiring people in their immediate geographical area. This opens up access to a much larger, global talent pool. For example, a tech startup in Silicon Valley can hire a software developer in India or a marketing expert in Germany without requiring them to relocate.

5. Improved Work-Life Balance: Remote work allows employees to manage their personal lives more effectively. They can attend to personal tasks during the day, such as doctor's appointments or family needs, without sacrificing work responsibilities. This helps in reducing stress and increasing job satisfaction. A remote worker may start work early, take a break to pick up their children from school, and then finish their work later in the evening.

1.4 Challenges of Remote Work

While remote work offers many benefits, it also comes with its own set of challenges that employees and employers need to address.

1. Communication Barriers: In a remote setting, face-to-face communication is limited, which can lead to misunderstandings or delays in decision-making. For instance, remote workers may miss non-verbal cues during virtual meetings, making it harder to interpret the tone or intent behind a message.

2. Isolation and Loneliness: Working from home can be isolating, especially for people who thrive on social interaction. Remote workers might miss out on the camaraderie and spontaneous interactions that come with working in an office. This can lead to feelings of loneliness. For example, a remote employee might feel disconnected from their colleagues if they rarely engage in team-building activities or casual conversations.

3. Work-Life Boundaries: When working remotely, the line between work and personal life can blur. Employees may find it difficult to "switch off" at the end of the day. For example, someone working from home might continue checking emails after their work hours or feel guilty about taking breaks, which can lead to burnout.

4. Distractions: While some workers may find fewer distractions at home, others might struggle to focus due to personal responsibilities, such as children, pets, or household chores. For instance, a remote worker with young children at home might need to juggle their professional responsibilities with childcare.

5. Technology Issues: Remote work heavily relies on technology, and technical issues can disrupt productivity. Unstable internet connections, outdated software, or cybersecurity concerns are common problems. For example, a remote worker could lose valuable work time if their internet connection drops during a critical video conference.

1.5 Remote Work Tools

A variety of digital tools have emerged to support remote work, making it easier for employees to communicate, collaborate, and manage projects effectively. Some popular remote work tools include:

1. Communication Tools: Platforms like Slack, Microsoft Teams, and Zoom are essential for staying in touch with colleagues and conducting virtual meetings. For example, a marketing team might use Slack to discuss ongoing campaigns or organize video calls for brainstorming sessions.

2. Project Management Tools: Tools like Trello, Asana, and Monday.com help teams manage tasks and projects efficiently. These platforms allow remote workers to assign tasks, set deadlines, and track progress in real-time. For instance, a remote web development team might use Asana to manage different stages of a website redesign project.

3. File Sharing and Collaboration: Cloud-based platforms such as Google Drive, Dropbox, and OneDrive enable remote teams to store and share files easily. These tools ensure that team members can collaborate on documents and access important files from any location. For example, a remote sales team could use Google Drive to share presentations and reports with clients.

4. Time Management Tools: Time-tracking software like Toggl and Clockify helps remote workers stay on top of their time management. These tools allow employees to track how much time they spend on different tasks, helping them stay productive and accountable.

5. Virtual Office Tools: Platforms like Sococo or Gather create virtual office environments, where team members can have casual conversations or quick meetings in a more immersive way, mimicking the physical office experience.

1.6 Examples of Remote Work in Action

To better understand how remote work operates, let's look at a few real-life examples:

- Example 1: A Digital Marketing Agency

Imagine a digital marketing agency that operates entirely remotely. The agency's employees are spread across multiple countries, with the CEO working from Los Angeles, the social media manager based in Brazil, and the content writers located in the UK and Canada. They use Slack to communicate daily, Asana to manage their marketing campaigns, and Google Drive to share content drafts and media files. Despite being in different time zones, they work cohesively through clear communication, weekly video meetings, and task management systems.

- Example 2: A Remote Customer Service Team

A customer service department for a global e-commerce company is fully remote. Customer service representatives work from home, answering customer queries via email, phone, or live chat. The company uses software like Zendesk to track customer inquiries and Zoom for regular training sessions. The representatives have flexible working hours, allowing them to assist customers around the world in different time zones.

- Example 3: Freelance Web Developer

A freelance web developer works remotely from various locations as they travel. They manage projects for clients using platforms like Upwork and communicate with clients through email and video calls. They use GitHub to collaborate on code with other developers and Google Calendar to schedule client meetings. This flexibility allows the developer to balance work and travel while maintaining high productivity levels.

Chapter 2

Setting Up Your Home Office

Working from home has become a common part of our lives. Whether you're a freelancer, running a business, or just working remotely, having a dedicated home office can boost your productivity and overall work satisfaction. In this chapter, we will discuss the key elements to consider when setting up your home office, including location, furniture, technology, and comfort. We will also provide examples to help guide you through the process.

1. Choosing the Right Location

The first step to creating a productive home office is choosing the right location. It's important to find a space in your home that offers privacy, minimizes distractions, and promotes focus.

Example 1: The Spare Room

If you have a spare room in your home, this can be the ideal space to set up your home office. It gives you a completely separate space where you can close the door and focus on your work without interruptions. This type of environment is especially useful if you share your home with others, such as family members or roommates.

Example 2: Corner of a Living Room

If you don't have a spare room, you can designate a corner of your living room or bedroom as your workspace. In this case, it's important to create a sense of separation between your work and home life. You can achieve this by using furniture to block off the space, such as a bookshelf or room divider, or even by just arranging your desk and chair in a way that faces away from distractions like the TV.

Key Tips for Choosing a Location:

- Privacy: If possible, pick a space where you can close the door to shut out noise and interruptions.

- Lighting: Look for a space with good natural light, as this can help reduce eye strain and boost your mood.

- Quiet: Choose a space that's far from noisy areas like the kitchen or living room.

2. Choosing the Right Furniture

After you've chosen the perfect spot for your home office, it's time to furnish it. The right furniture can make or break your comfort and productivity, so it's essential to invest in key pieces like a desk and an ergonomic chair.

Example 1: Traditional Desk and Ergonomic Chair

The classic setup includes a desk with enough surface space for your computer, paperwork, and any other materials you might need. Pair this with an ergonomic chair that supports your back and promotes good posture. For example, the IKEA Bekant desk offers an adjustable height feature, making it easy to switch between sitting and standing. The Herman Miller Aeron chair is a popular ergonomic choice, known for its adjustable armrests, lumbar support, and breathable material.

Example 2: Standing Desk

Standing desks have become popular in recent years due to their health benefits, including reducing the risks associated with sitting for long periods. A standing desk, like the Flexispot Electric Standing Desk, allows you to alternate between sitting and standing, which can improve your posture and energy levels throughout the day.

Example 3: Compact Fold-Out Desk

For smaller spaces, a fold-out desk can be an excellent solution. For instance, the Fold Out Convertible Desk from Wayfair provides a sleek design that folds up when not in use, saving space and keeping your home clutter-free.

Key Tips for Choosing Furniture:

- Comfort: Invest in an ergonomic chair and a desk that suits your working needs.

- Space Efficiency: Choose furniture that fits comfortably in your designated office space without crowding it.

- Storage: Consider adding shelves or filing cabinets to keep your work organized.

3. Technology and Equipment

To function efficiently, your home office needs to be equipped with the right technology. This includes your computer, internet connection, printer, and any other devices essential for your work.

Example 1: Computer Setup

If you work primarily on a computer, it's worth investing in a setup that is both functional and comfortable. A dual-monitor setup can enhance your productivity by allowing you to multitask more effectively. For example, a content writer might use one screen for researching and the other for writing.

Example 2: High-Speed Internet

A reliable internet connection is crucial for remote work. Make sure your Wi-Fi is fast and stable, especially if you're attending virtual meetings or need to download/upload large files. If your internet connection is slow or unreliable, consider upgrading your plan or investing in a mesh Wi-Fi system like Google Nest Wi-Fi, which can help eliminate dead zones in your home.

Example 3: Printer and Scanner

Depending on your work, you may need access to a printer or scanner. A multifunction printer like the HP OfficeJet Pro 9025 is a great all-in-one solution, offering printing, scanning, copying, and faxing capabilities.

Key Tips for Setting Up Technology:

- Internet: Make sure your internet connection is strong enough for video calls, file sharing, and cloud services.

- Backup Power: Consider using a surge protector or an uninterruptible power supply (UPS) to protect your equipment from power surges.

- Cable Management: Keep your workspace tidy by organizing your cables with clips or cable ties.

4. Creating a Comfortable Environment

One of the advantages of working from home is the ability to create a workspace that is truly comfortable. Consider the temperature, lighting, and overall atmosphere of your home office to ensure that it's a place where you can focus and feel good about spending time.

Example 1: Temperature Control

A comfortable temperature is essential for staying focused. If your home office tends to get too hot or too cold, consider using a space heater or a fan to regulate the temperature. Smart thermostats, like the Nest Thermostat, allow you to set and control the temperature of your home office without leaving your desk.

Example 2: Lighting

Good lighting is key to maintaining focus and preventing eye strain. Natural light is best, but if your office doesn't get much sunlight, invest in good-quality artificial lighting. A desk lamp with adjustable brightness, like the TaoTronics LED Desk Lamp, can help you create the perfect lighting for different times of the day.

Example 3: Personalizing Your Space

Since this is your personal workspace, don't be afraid to add a touch of personality. Decorate your office with items that inspire you, such as plants, artwork, or motivational quotes. A small plant like a snake plant or a peace lily can add a bit of greenery and improve air quality. If you enjoy listening to music while you work, consider investing in a Bluetooth speaker or noise-canceling headphones, like the Bose QuietComfort series, to create the perfect sound environment.

Key Tips for Creating a Comfortable Environment:

- Lighting: Use a mix of natural and artificial lighting to keep your workspace well-lit.

- Temperature: Ensure your workspace is at a comfortable temperature throughout the day.

- Personal Touch: Add decor and accessories that make the space feel uniquely yours.

5. Organizing Your Space for Efficiency

An organized workspace leads to an organized mind. Make sure that your home office is set up in a way that promotes efficiency and keeps your work materials easily accessible.

Example 1: Storage Solutions

If you have a lot of paperwork or office supplies, invest in organizational tools like filing cabinets, drawer organizers, or shelving units. For instance, the IKEA Kallax shelving unit is both stylish and functional, providing ample storage space for books, files, and decorative items.

Example 2: Cable Management

A cluttered desk can make it harder to focus. Use cable management tools like clips, trays, or even a simple Velcro strip to keep cords and cables neatly organized. This not only helps maintain a clean aesthetic but also makes it easier to find and plug in your devices when needed.

Example 3: Task Management Tools

Digital organization is just as important as physical organization. Tools like Trello or Asana can help you keep track of tasks, deadlines, and projects, ensuring that you stay on top of your workload.

Key Tips for Organizing Your Space:

- Declutter: Keep only essential items on your desk to maintain a clean, organized workspace.

- Storage: Use drawers, shelves, and bins to keep paperwork and supplies organized and out of sight.

- Digital Tools: Use task management software to organize your workload and avoid feeling overwhelmed.

Chapter 3

Finding Your Niche

In the world of entrepreneurship and business, "finding your niche" is one of the most important steps to success. It involves identifying a specific segment of the market that you can serve effectively and distinctively. When done correctly, it allows you to focus your efforts, gain a competitive edge, and build a loyal customer base.

In this chapter, we will explore the concept of finding your niche, why it's crucial, and how to identify your niche with examples.

What Is a Niche?

A niche is essentially a specialized market within a larger industry. It refers to a specific group of people who have particular needs, preferences, or problems that are not fully addressed by the broader market. By catering to a smaller, more targeted group, businesses can become experts in meeting those needs.

For example:
- Industry: Fitness
- Niche: Yoga for seniors
- Industry: Food
- Niche: Vegan desserts for people with gluten allergies

When a business serves a niche, it can become the go-to resource for that specific audience, building trust and authority in that space.

Why Is Finding a Niche Important?

Finding your niche offers several benefits:

1. Reduced Competition: By narrowing your focus, you face less competition. Instead of trying to appeal to everyone, you tailor your products or services to a particular group, giving you a competitive advantage.

2. Stronger Customer Loyalty: When customers feel that a product or service is designed specifically for them, they are more likely to become loyal customers.

3. Improved Marketing Efficiency: With a clear understanding of your target audience, you can create more precise marketing messages, focusing on the needs and interests of a particular group.

4. Increased Profitability: Specializing in a niche allows businesses to often charge premium prices because customers value the expertise and specialized services or products they receive.

Steps to Finding Your Niche

1. Identify Your Interests and Passions

To start, think about your own interests and passions. It's much easier to build a business around something you enjoy or care about. Plus, when you're passionate about your niche, you'll have more motivation and creativity to keep going, even when challenges arise.

Example: If you love gardening and spend your weekends planting flowers, your niche could be related to urban gardening, organic fertilizers, or plant care tips for beginners.

2. Analyze Market Demand

While passion is important, it's not enough. You also need to ensure there's demand for your niche. Look for existing problems or gaps in the market that need to be addressed.

One way to analyze demand is to use online tools like Google Trends or keyword research platforms to see what people are searching for. You can also browse forums, social media groups, or review sites to find out what challenges people are facing and how they describe their needs.

Example: Imagine you love photography. You could discover that there's a growing interest in drone photography for real estate agents who need aerial shots of properties. If there aren't many services offering this locally, that could be a profitable niche.

3. Assess Your Skills and Strengths

Next, think about your skills and strengths. What are you particularly good at? Combining your passion with your skills will give you a greater chance of success.

If you have a skill set that complements your passion, you'll be able to offer something unique in the market. This could be anything from your experience in customer service, technical expertise, or artistic talent.

Example: If you're a certified nutritionist and you're passionate about wellness, your niche might be developing personalized nutrition plans for new moms or people with specific dietary restrictions.

4. Research Your Competition

Once you have a potential niche in mind, research your competition. Look at businesses that are already operating in your niche and analyze what they offer, how they market themselves, and how successful they are.

While competition isn't necessarily a bad thing, you don't want to enter a market that's already saturated. Instead, look for gaps in their offerings or underserved segments of the market.

Example: If you notice that many skincare brands offer organic products but few focus specifically on eco-friendly packaging, you might choose to develop a line of sustainable skincare products that use only recyclable or biodegradable materials.

5. Define Your Unique Selling Proposition (USP)

Your USP is what makes you stand out from the competition. It's the special value you offer that no one else does. To define your USP, consider the following:

- What problem are you solving for your niche audience?

- What unique experience or skills do you bring to the table?

- How can you deliver better or different results than others?

Example: Let's say you want to offer yoga classes. There are countless yoga instructors out there, but your USP could be "Yoga for Busy Professionals," offering short, 20-minute sessions specifically designed to fit into the hectic schedules of working people.

6. Test Your Idea

Before you fully commit to your niche, it's wise to test the waters. You don't need to invest a lot of money or time to do this. You can start by offering your product or service on a small scale to see how people respond.

This might involve launching a simple website, offering a free workshop, or creating a few sample products. Gather feedback from your target audience and see if they find value in what you're offering.

Example: If your niche is "vegan desserts for people with gluten allergies," you could start by offering your desserts at a local farmers market or hosting tasting events. This will help you gauge interest and adjust your offerings based on customer feedback.

7. Stay Flexible

As you dive into your niche, it's important to stay flexible. Sometimes, you may need to pivot or slightly adjust your focus based on market trends or customer feedback. Being adaptable will help you thrive in your niche and keep up with changes in your industry.

Example: Perhaps you start by offering vegan desserts, but later you discover that customers are more interested in gluten-free savory snacks. By listening to your audience and adapting to their preferences, you can refine your niche and build a more successful business.

Examples of Successful Niche Businesses

Let's look at some real-world examples of successful niche businesses to inspire you:

- Lush Cosmetics: This brand has carved out a niche in the beauty industry by focusing on handmade, cruelty-free cosmetics with minimal packaging. Their commitment to ethical practices has earned them a loyal customer base, even in a highly competitive market.

- Dollar Shave Club: Rather than trying to compete with large razor brands in traditional stores, Dollar Shave Club found a niche by offering affordable razors delivered to customers' doors through a subscription model. Their clever marketing and focus on convenience helped them stand out.

- The Honest Company: Founded by actress Jessica Alba, The Honest Company focuses on selling eco-friendly, non-toxic baby and household products. They serve a niche market of parents who prioritize sustainability and safety in their purchasing decisions.

- Tiny House Builders: As more people look to downsize and live minimally, the tiny house movement has gained popularity. Tiny house builders have found a niche in designing and constructing compact, efficient homes for people who want to live with less.

To summarize:

1. Identify your passions and interests.

2. Research market demand and competition.

3. Leverage your skills and strengths.

4. Define your unique selling proposition (USP).

5. Test your niche idea with your target audience.

6. Stay flexible and open to adjustments.

Remember, the key to success in any niche is staying focused on the needs of your specific audience and continually providing them with value. As long as you're meeting those needs, your niche business has the potential to grow and prosper.

Chapter 4

Building Your Portfolio

Your portfolio is a crucial element of your professional identity. Whether you're an artist, a designer, a writer, or a developer, a strong portfolio showcases your skills, accomplishments, and versatility. Building a portfolio might seem daunting at first, but with a clear plan and structure, you can craft a powerful portfolio that tells the story of your professional journey.

In this chapter, we'll explore the steps to building a portfolio, provide examples of how to display your work effectively, and offer tips to ensure it stands out.

Why Do You Need a Portfolio?

A portfolio serves as more than just a collection of your work. It's your personal brand and a visual representation of your abilities and growth. Employers, clients, or collaborators often use your portfolio to assess your style, creativity, and range.

For example, if you're a graphic designer, your portfolio can display your ability to work with different types of media, such as print, digital, or branding projects. It will give potential employers or clients a sense of whether your skills match their needs.

A good portfolio should:
- Highlight your best work.
- Demonstrate your growth over time.

- Showcase a variety of skills.

- Convey your unique style or approach.

Types of Portfolios

There are many types of portfolios depending on your field of work. Below are a few common examples:

1. Creative Portfolios (Artists, Designers, Photographers)

- Contains visuals such as illustrations, designs, photographs, and even animations. Each piece should be clearly labeled, with descriptions explaining your role and the project's context.

- Example: A freelance photographer may have categories like "Weddings," "Portraits," and "Landscape Photography," with curated images in each section.

2. Writing Portfolios (Content Creators, Authors, Journalists)

- Focuses on written samples, showcasing your ability to write for different audiences and in different formats, like blogs, articles, copywriting, or creative writing.

- Example: A content writer may organize their portfolio by subject, including samples of blog posts, website content, and social media campaigns.

3. Development Portfolios (Software Developers, Web Designers)

- Showcases projects that highlight your technical skills. This often includes links to live projects, code repositories (e.g., GitHub), and project descriptions that detail your role and the tools you used.

- Example: A web developer might have a section for each major project, showing screenshots of websites they've built, along with brief explanations of their contribution.

4. Academic Portfolios (Students, Researchers, Educators)

- Used to present academic achievements, including research papers, presentations, and teaching materials.

- Example: A researcher may organize their portfolio into categories like "Published Papers," "Research Proposals," and "Conference Presentations."

Steps to Building Your Portfolio

1. Define Your Goals and Audience

Before you start gathering material for your portfolio, you need to define your purpose and audience. Are you targeting employers, clients, or collaborators? What specific skills do you want to showcase? Your portfolio should reflect your goals and be tailored to the type of opportunities you are seeking.

- Example: If you're a graphic designer aiming to get a job in advertising, your portfolio should highlight branding projects, ad designs, and creative campaigns. If you're looking to freelance, you might want to showcase a variety of projects that show versatility across industries.

2. Select Your Best Work

Quality always trumps quantity in a portfolio. It's tempting to include everything you've ever worked on, but a cluttered portfolio can dilute the impact of your strongest pieces. Focus on your best work that aligns with your goals and demonstrates a range of skills.

- Example: If you're a writer, include a mix of long-form articles, short blogs, and social media content. This demonstrates your versatility across different platforms. For developers, a project that shows your problem-solving skills is more impactful than a simple website clone.

Tips:

- Limit your portfolio to 8–12 pieces of work.

- Prioritize recent work, but don't hesitate to include older pieces if they are particularly strong or relevant.

- Avoid including unfinished projects unless they still showcase a valuable skill or concept.

3. Describe Each Project

A portfolio is not just a visual display; it should provide context for each piece of work. Descriptions help viewers understand the thought process, challenges, and skills that went into a project.

For each project, include:

- The client or context (was it for a personal project, client, or employer?)

- Your role in the project (what were your specific contributions?)

- The tools and technologies you used (e.g., Adobe Photoshop, JavaScript, WordPress)

- Any results or impact (did it increase sales, engagement, etc.?)

- Example (Graphic Designer):

- Project: Redesign of a local bakery's brand identity.

- Role: Lead designer responsible for logo, packaging, and promotional materials.

- Tools: Adobe Illustrator, Photoshop.

- Results: Helped the bakery increase foot traffic by 25% in the first month after the rebrand.

4. Organize and Structure Your Portfolio

An organized portfolio is easier to navigate and more pleasant for viewers to explore. Think of it like a website—make it user-friendly with clear sections and navigation.

Tips:

- Categorize your work based on the type of project (e.g., graphic design, web development, photography).

- Use a simple, consistent layout across all projects to maintain professionalism.

- Ensure that projects are organized in a logical order—your most impressive work should be at the top.

- Example (Web Developer Portfolio):

- Homepage with a brief introduction.

- A "Projects" section divided into categories like "Web Design," "App Development," and "UI/UX Design."

- Each project page contains screenshots, a project description, and a link to the live project or code repository.

5. Choose the Right Platform

Your portfolio's platform is as important as the content itself. Depending on your field, you have different options for displaying your work. Here are a few popular choices:

- Personal Website: A personalized website gives you the most control over your portfolio's appearance and structure. It can also include other elements, like an "About Me" page, testimonials, and a blog.

- Example Platforms: WordPress, Wix, Squarespace.

- Portfolio Hosting Websites: These sites make it easy to showcase your work without needing to build a site from scratch.

- Example Platforms: Behance (for creatives), Dribbble (for designers), GitHub (for developers).

- PDF or Physical Portfolio: For certain industries like architecture or interior design, having a PDF or physical portfolio may be necessary for in-person presentations. Make sure it's visually cohesive and organized.

6. Keep Your Portfolio Updated

As you complete new projects and gain more experience, your portfolio should grow alongside you. Set a reminder to review and update your portfolio every few months, removing outdated work and adding fresh, relevant pieces.

- Example: A software developer who has recently learned React might update their portfolio with new projects that demonstrate their React skills, while removing older, less-relevant projects.

Examples of Strong Portfolios

Let's look at some examples of how different professionals can create strong portfolios:

- Graphic Designer Example:

- Sarah's portfolio is neatly organized into sections like "Branding," "Web Design," and "Illustrations." Each project has a title, a description, and a breakdown of her role. Sarah includes high-quality images and provides links to live websites when applicable. Her portfolio's aesthetic matches her design style, giving potential clients a clear understanding of her skills and taste.

- Software Developer Example:

- Mike's portfolio highlights his skills in web development. His projects include links to live sites, along with GitHub repositories where potential employers can review his code. Each project is accompanied by a description of the technology stack (e.g., HTML, CSS, JavaScript) and what challenges he solved during development.

Final Thoughts

Building a strong portfolio is an ongoing process. Your portfolio should grow as your skills and experiences develop. Remember to focus on quality over quantity, provide clear context for each project, and tailor your portfolio to your audience. A well-crafted portfolio not only showcases your best work but also tells the story of your career.

Now that you know how to build your portfolio, start gathering your best work and get started today! Your portfolio is your key to standing out in a competitive job market or attracting new clients.

Chapter 5

Finding Clients

In any business, especially a service-based one, finding clients is the lifeblood of success. Without clients, it doesn't matter how skilled or talented you are; your business won't thrive. In this chapter, we'll explore practical and effective strategies for finding clients, even if you're just starting out. The goal is to make this process simple and actionable, so you can start building relationships and growing your business immediately.

1. Define Your Ideal Client

The first step to finding clients is knowing who you want to serve. This helps you focus your energy on people who are most likely to need and value what you offer.

What Is an Ideal Client?

An ideal client is someone who:

- Needs your product or service
- Can afford to pay for it
- Will benefit from your skills or offerings
- Aligns with your business values

Let's say you're a freelance graphic designer. Your ideal client might be small business owners who need branding materials, such as logos or social media graphics, but can't afford a full-fledged design agency. They need something professional yet affordable.

Example:

Imagine Sarah, a freelance web developer, specializes in building websites for local cafes and restaurants. Her ideal clients are small cafe owners who want a simple but functional website to showcase their menu and attract customers. By focusing on these business owners, Sarah can tailor her marketing and communication to appeal directly to them.

2. Leverage Your Network

One of the easiest ways to find clients is by tapping into the people you already know. Often, the best clients come from personal recommendations. Don't underestimate the power of your current network—friends, family, colleagues, or even past employers.

Steps to Leverage Your Network:

- Let everyone know what you do: Share your services with your personal and professional contacts, whether through a simple message, email, or social media post.

- Ask for referrals: Tell your network you're looking for clients, and ask if they know anyone who might need your services.

- Offer incentives: Sometimes offering a small discount or a referral fee can encourage people to recommend your services to others.

Example:

John is a freelance photographer who specializes in event photography. He reached out to a former colleague who worked at a corporate company and offered his services. That colleague mentioned John to their event coordinator, leading to several bookings for corporate events.

3. Use Online Platforms

In today's digital age, there are plenty of online platforms where clients are actively looking for freelancers and businesses. These platforms are especially helpful when you're just starting out, as they provide easy access to potential clients who are already searching for the services you offer.

Popular Platforms:

- Upwork: A freelance platform where clients post projects, and freelancers bid on jobs.

- Fiverr: Freelancers list their services, often at a starting price of $5, and clients can directly hire them.

- LinkedIn: This professional social network allows you to connect with potential clients, showcase your work, and join relevant groups or forums.

- Freelancer: Another popular freelance job board, where you can browse and bid on projects.

Example:

Lisa is a virtual assistant who wanted to expand her client base. She created a profile on Upwork, highlighting her skills in email management, customer support, and scheduling. Within a few weeks, she landed her first client and, through consistent effort, built a steady stream of work from the platform.

4. Build a Portfolio Website

A portfolio website is a powerful tool to showcase your work and attract clients. It serves as a digital resume where potential clients can see examples of your work, learn about your services, and easily contact you.

What to Include in a Portfolio Website:

- About Me: Introduce yourself and your business. Let people know your background, expertise, and what sets you apart from others.

- Services: Clearly list the services you offer. Be specific about what clients can expect when working with you.

- Portfolio: Showcase your best work. This could be designs, case studies, testimonials, or previous projects you've completed.

- Contact Info: Make it easy for potential clients to reach you by including a contact form, email address, or phone number.

Example:

Tom is a freelance graphic designer. He built a simple website showcasing his design work, including logos, brochures, and website layouts. When potential clients visit his site, they can see his style, read about his design process, and contact him for inquiries. Over time, Tom's website helped him attract clients who were impressed with his previous work and professionalism.

5. Use Social Media

Social media platforms like Instagram, Facebook, Twitter, and LinkedIn are great for finding clients, especially if you're consistent and strategic in your approach. Each platform offers unique ways to engage with potential clients and showcase your expertise.

Social Media Strategies:

- Instagram: If you have a visual business, such as photography, graphic design, or fashion, Instagram is perfect for sharing your work. Post regularly, use relevant hashtags, and engage with your followers.

- LinkedIn: Use LinkedIn to connect with potential clients in your industry. Share content related to your services, join relevant groups, and engage in discussions.

- Facebook Groups: Join groups where your ideal clients might hang out. Offer advice, share valuable content, and position yourself as a helpful expert without directly pitching your services right away.

Example:

Marie is a content writer who uses LinkedIn to find clients. She regularly posts tips on effective writing and content strategy, and she connects with business owners who need help with blog writing. Through consistent posting and engagement, Marie has built a network of potential clients who reach out to her when they need content written.

6. Cold Emailing

While cold emailing can seem intimidating, it's a proven method for finding clients. A well-crafted email to a potential client can result in new business opportunities.

Tips for Effective Cold Emails:

- Personalize the message: Do your research and tailor the email to each client. Mention their business or a specific project you admire.

- Be clear and concise: Get straight to the point. Explain who you are, what you offer, and how you can solve a problem for the client.

- Offer value: Don't just ask for work; offer something of value, such as a free consultation, an audit, or helpful tips related to their business.

- Follow up: If you don't get a response right away, send a polite follow-up email a few days later.

Example:

David is a web developer who specializes in creating websites for local restaurants. He researched small, independent restaurants in his area and sent them personalized cold emails, offering a free website audit. His emails were short and highlighted how he could improve their online presence. As a result, David secured a few meetings, leading to new clients.

7. Attend Networking Events

Networking events, both in-person and virtual, are excellent opportunities to meet potential clients and build relationships. These events allow you to introduce yourself, share what you do, and form connections that could turn into business opportunities.

Types of Networking Events:

- Industry Conferences: Attend conferences in your industry to meet people who might need your services.

- Local Business Meetups: Check out local meetups or business groups where small business owners gather. These are great places to meet potential clients.

- Online Webinars and Workshops: Many industries offer online networking events or webinars where you can meet potential clients virtually.

Example:

Emma is a social media manager who attended a digital marketing conference. She met several small business owners who needed help with their social media strategies. By following up with them after the event, Emma was able to secure a few new clients.

8. Collaborate with Other Businesses

Collaborating with other businesses can help you find new clients and expand your reach. Partnering with complementary businesses allows you to tap into their client base, and they can refer clients to you.

Ideas for Collaboration:

- Joint ventures: Partner with a business that complements yours. For example, a web developer might partner with a graphic designer to offer a complete website package.

- Referrals: Build relationships with businesses that target the same audience as you. For example, a personal trainer might team up with a nutritionist to refer clients to each other.

- Guest blogging or podcasts: Offer to write guest blog posts or appear on podcasts hosted by businesses that serve your ideal clients. This helps you reach a new audience and position yourself as an expert.

Example:

Kelly is a freelance writer who partnered with a graphic designer to offer website copy and design packages for small businesses. By working together, they were able to attract more clients and offer a complete service that was more appealing to their target audience.

Conclusion: Finding Clients is About Building Relationships

The key to finding clients isn't just about selling—it's about building relationships. Whether through networking, online platforms, cold emails, or social media, the goal is to create genuine connections with people who need your services. Focus on offering value, showcasing your expertise, and staying consistent in your efforts. Over time, these relationships will help you build a steady stream of clients and grow your business.

Chapter 6

Pitching and Proposals

In any business or career, communication is crucial, especially when it comes to pitching ideas or presenting proposals. Whether you're an entrepreneur trying to secure funding, a freelancer seeking new clients, or a professional hoping to win a project, the ability to present your ideas effectively can determine your success. This chapter will help you understand how to craft compelling pitches and proposals and provide examples to make your learning experience practical.

What is a Pitch?

A pitch is a concise, persuasive message that explains an idea or product. The purpose of a pitch is to quickly grab attention and spark interest. Typically, a pitch is used to introduce a new concept, business, or product to potential investors, clients, or collaborators. A good pitch is simple yet powerful, highlighting the core aspects of your idea and why it's valuable.

Types of Pitches

1. Elevator Pitch: This is a brief pitch (usually around 30 seconds to 2 minutes) designed to be delivered in the time it takes for a short elevator ride. It's a quick summary of who you are, what you offer, and why someone should care.

Example:

Imagine you're an app developer pitching your idea in an elevator with a potential investor.

"Hi, I'm Jane, founder of EcoFriend, an app that helps users track and reduce their carbon footprint in daily life. With personalized tips and community challenges, we've already helped 10,000 users reduce their emissions by 20%. We're seeking $100,000 to scale up and add more features. Would you be open to discussing this further?"

2. Investor Pitch: This is more in-depth than an elevator pitch and is used when seeking funding or investment. It typically includes a detailed explanation of the product, market opportunity, business model, and financials.

Example:

You're an entrepreneur pitching to venture capitalists for your startup.

"EcoFriend is an app designed to help individuals and businesses reduce their carbon footprint by tracking and optimizing daily activities. Our app has seen tremendous growth, with over 10,000 users in the first six months. We generate revenue through premium subscriptions and partnerships with eco-friendly brands. We're seeking $500,000 in seed funding to expand our features and scale marketing efforts, with a projected user base of 100,000 in the next year. With increasing awareness of climate change, we believe there's a significant opportunity to grow in this space."

3. Sales Pitch: A sales pitch is used when selling a product or service to potential customers. It's focused on the value the product brings to the customer and how it solves their specific problems.

Example:

You're a freelancer pitching your web design services to a small business owner.

"Hi, I'm Alex, a web designer specializing in small business websites. I noticed your site is a bit outdated, which might be turning away potential customers. I can help you redesign it to make it more modern, mobile-friendly, and optimized for search engines. With a new design, you could see a 30% increase in traffic and engagement. Would you be interested in discussing how I can help?"

Key Elements of a Pitch

1. Introduction: Start by introducing yourself or your company. Keep it brief but memorable.

2. Problem Statement: Clearly identify the problem you're solving. This helps the listener understand the relevance of your idea.

3. Solution: Present your product, service, or idea as the solution to the problem.

4. Value Proposition: Explain why your solution is better than others. Highlight the benefits and how it creates value for the listener.

5. Call to Action: End with a clear call to action, such as requesting a meeting, further discussion, or support.

What is a Proposal?

A proposal is a formal document that outlines an offer, plan, or project. Proposals are usually more detailed than pitches and are often required for larger projects, contracts, or collaborations. The goal of a proposal is to convince the recipient to approve or support your plan.

Types of Proposals

1. Business Proposal: This is a detailed plan for a project or partnership. It often includes a breakdown of costs, timelines, and deliverables.

Example:

You're a marketing consultant submitting a proposal to a company to improve their digital presence.

"Our proposal for enhancing your online visibility includes a comprehensive strategy to increase web traffic by 50% in six months. We will redesign your website, optimize your content for SEO, and launch targeted social media campaigns. The project timeline is six months, with a total cost of $25,000, including all services and support. Detailed milestones and expected results are outlined in the attached document."

2. Grant Proposal: Used by non-profits or researchers to secure funding from governments, organizations, or foundations for specific projects.

<hr>

EXAMPLE:

You're part of a non-profit organization seeking funding for a community garden project.

"We propose creating a community garden to improve food security in our neighborhood. This project will provide fresh produce to 200 families and educational workshops on sustainable gardening. We are seeking $10,000 in grant funding to cover the costs of land, tools, and educational materials. The project will be completed in one year, and detailed budgeting is provided in the appendix."

3. Project Proposal: This is used within a company or organization when planning internal projects or initiatives. It includes a breakdown of goals, timelines, and required resources.

Example:

You're proposing a new employee training program to your HR department.

"Our proposal is to implement a new employee onboarding program to improve productivity and retention. The program will provide comprehensive training on company policies, tools, and culture within the first 30 days of hire. The project will take three months to develop and will require $5,000 in software and training resources. By investing in this program, we expect to reduce new employee turnover by 25%."

Key Elements of a Proposal

1. Executive Summary: A brief overview of the entire proposal. It should summarize the key points and entice the reader to continue.

2. Introduction: Provide context for the proposal, including background information on the problem or need you're addressing.

3. Goals and Objectives: Clearly outline the specific goals and objectives of the proposal. What do you hope to achieve?

4. Plan of Action: Describe the steps you will take to accomplish the goals. This should include timelines, resources, and deliverables.

5. Budget/Costs: Include a breakdown of costs, whether it's for services, materials, or other expenses.

6. Benefits/Value: Highlight the benefits of your proposal and how it will add value to the recipient.

7. Conclusion: End with a strong conclusion that reinforces the value of your proposal and includes a call to action, such as scheduling a meeting or next steps.

Tips for Successful Pitches and Proposals

1. Know Your Audience: Tailor your pitch or proposal to the specific needs and interests of your audience. What do they care about most? Speak directly to those concerns.

2. Keep It Clear and Concise: Avoid jargon or overly technical language. Make sure your message is easy to understand, even for someone unfamiliar with your field.

3. Tell a Story: People connect with stories. Use storytelling techniques to make your pitch or proposal more engaging. For example, you could describe how your idea helped someone or improved a situation.

4. Provide Evidence: Back up your claims with data, examples, or testimonials. If you're pitching a product, demonstrate its success or potential with real-world results.

5. Practice: For pitches, especially, practice is essential. Rehearse your pitch until it feels natural and you can deliver it confidently, even under pressure.

6. Be Confident, but Not Arrogant: Confidence is key to selling your idea, but avoid coming across as too aggressive or boastful. Show humility while still demonstrating that you believe in your idea.

Common Mistakes to Avoid

1. Being Too Vague: Whether in a pitch or proposal, avoid being too general or vague about your ideas. Be specific about what you're offering and the results you expect.

2. Focusing Too Much on Yourself: While it's important to present your qualifications or the value of your product, always frame it in terms of how it benefits the recipient. Avoid making it all about you.

3. Overloading with Information: Especially in a pitch, don't overwhelm your audience with too much information at once. Focus on the core points and be concise.

4. Ignoring Follow-Up: After delivering a pitch or submitting a proposal, always follow up. This shows professionalism and keeps the conversation going.

⎯⎯●⎯⎯

BY MASTERING THE ART of pitching and proposals, you'll be well-equipped to present your ideas effectively, win new opportunities, and build stronger business relationships. Remember, both pitching and proposing are skills that improve with practice, so keep refining your approach, learning from feedback, and adapting to your audience's needs.

Chapter 7

Time Management and Productivity

Time management and productivity are two sides of the same coin. The better you manage your time, the more productive you become. However, achieving this balance is often easier said than done. In today's world, distractions are everywhere, and tasks can pile up, leading to stress and burnout. In this chapter, we'll explore the importance of time management and offer practical tips on how you can improve your productivity with examples to guide you.

What is Time Management?

Time management refers to the process of planning and controlling how much time you spend on specific activities. It's about working smarter, not harder. The ultimate goal is to maximize the effectiveness of your efforts, so you can achieve your goals in less time and with less stress.

Time management is not about cramming as many tasks as possible into your day. Rather, it's about using your time wisely and effectively. When you manage your time well, you can prioritize tasks, minimize distractions, and make more informed decisions about how to spend your day.

Why is Time Management Important?

1. Reduces Stress: When you know what needs to be done and when, you can stay organized and feel more in control. This reduces stress and anxiety.

2. Increases Productivity: Good time management allows you to accomplish more in a shorter amount of time. By focusing on key tasks, you can make the most of every minute.

3. Improves Work-Life Balance: Effective time management leaves room for both work and personal activities. You'll have more time to spend with family, pursue hobbies, and relax.

4. Boosts Confidence: When you successfully manage your time and complete tasks, you gain a sense of accomplishment and boost your confidence.

Common Time Management Challenges

Before diving into strategies, it's important to recognize some common time management challenges that many people face.

- Procrastination: Putting off tasks until the last minute leads to poor performance and increased stress.

- Multitasking: While many people believe multitasking is productive, it often leads to mistakes and slower progress.

- Distractions: In today's digital world, distractions such as social media, emails, and notifications are constant.

- Poor Prioritization: Focusing on less important tasks first can lead to an imbalance, where crucial tasks are neglected.

Time Management Techniques

Let's explore some effective time management techniques that will help you make the most of your day.

1. The Pomodoro Technique

The Pomodoro Technique is a popular method for staying focused. It involves breaking your workday into 25-minute intervals, known as "Pomodoros," followed by a 5-minute break. After completing four Pomodoros, you take a longer break of 15–30 minutes.

This technique works because it keeps you focused on one task at a time. It also gives your brain regular breaks, which helps maintain your energy levels throughout the day.

Example:

Sarah has a report due at the end of the day. Instead of working on it continuously for hours, she sets a timer for 25 minutes and works solely on the report. After the 25 minutes, she takes a short 5-minute break to stretch and relax. She repeats this cycle and finishes her report without feeling overwhelmed.

2. The Eisenhower Matrix

The Eisenhower Matrix helps you prioritize tasks based on urgency and importance. It divides tasks into four quadrants:

- Urgent and Important: Do these tasks immediately.

- Important but Not Urgent: Schedule time to do these tasks.

- Urgent but Not Important: Delegate these tasks to others if possible.

- Neither Urgent Nor Important: Eliminate or postpone these tasks.

This technique helps you focus on what truly matters, rather than wasting time on trivial tasks.

Example:

John is preparing for a big presentation, but his inbox is flooded with emails. Using the Eisenhower Matrix, he decides to focus on finishing his presentation (Important but Not Urgent) and delegate email sorting to his assistant (Urgent but Not Important). This allows him to stay focused on the task that will have the most significant impact.

3. Time Blocking

Time blocking involves scheduling specific blocks of time for different tasks or activities. It helps you stay on track and ensures you dedicate the right amount of time to each task. By assigning a specific time for each task, you prevent one activity from eating up too much of your day.

Example:

Maria works as a graphic designer. To avoid spending all day on one project, she blocks off her morning (9 AM - 12 PM) for client work. After lunch, she blocks time from 1 PM to 3 PM for personal development and from 3 PM to 5 PM for administrative tasks like responding to emails. This structure helps her maintain a balance between client work and her personal growth.

4. The Two-Minute Rule

If a task takes less than two minutes to complete, do it immediately. This is the Two-Minute Rule. Many small tasks can be quickly dealt with, and postponing them often causes unnecessary clutter in your to-do list.

Example:

Mark receives a quick request to send a document to his colleague. Instead of adding it to his list of things to do later, he takes 30 seconds to send the file immediately, allowing him to focus on bigger tasks without this lingering in the back of his mind.

5. The Pareto Principle (80/20 Rule)

The Pareto Principle states that 80% of results come from 20% of your efforts. Focus on the 20% of tasks that yield the most significant outcomes. By identifying and prioritizing the most impactful tasks, you can significantly increase your productivity.

Example:

Lisa runs an online business. She realizes that 80% of her revenue comes from 20% of her clients. She decides to focus on nurturing those key relationships rather than spreading herself too thin across smaller clients. As a result, her revenue increases without additional work.

Staying Productive: Tips and Strategies

Time management techniques are only part of the equation. You also need to stay productive, even when motivation is low. Here are some tips to keep your productivity levels high:

1. Set SMART Goals

SMART goals are specific, measurable, achievable, relevant, and time-bound. When you have clear and realistic goals, it's easier to stay motivated and focused.

Example:

Instead of saying, "I want to finish my project soon," you can set a SMART goal like, "I will complete the first draft of my project by 5 PM on Friday." This gives you a specific timeline and a measurable outcome.

2. Limit Distractions

Distractions can derail your productivity. Identify the things that distract you most, whether it's your phone, social media, or coworkers, and take steps to minimize them.

Example:

David finds that he spends too much time checking social media. He decides to put his phone on "Do Not Disturb" mode during work hours and only check his social media accounts during his breaks. This small change significantly improves his focus and productivity.

3. Take Breaks

Regular breaks are essential for maintaining productivity throughout the day. Short breaks allow your brain to recharge, preventing burnout and keeping your energy levels up.

Example:

Jessica schedules short breaks after every 90 minutes of work. During these breaks, she goes for a quick walk or grabs a coffee. This helps her stay energized and avoids the mid-afternoon slump.

4. Review and Reflect

At the end of each day or week, take some time to review your progress and reflect on what you've accomplished. This helps you identify areas for improvement and stay motivated for future tasks.

Example:

Michael reviews his to-do list every evening. He checks off completed tasks and notes any challenges he faced. This reflection helps him make adjustments to his schedule for the next day and continuously improve his time management skills.

5. Use Technology Wisely

There are many tools and apps available that can help you stay organized and productive. From task management apps like Trello or Asana to time-tracking apps like Toggl, technology can help you stay on top of your tasks.

Example:

Emma uses a project management tool to keep track of her team's progress. Each task is assigned a deadline, and the tool sends her reminders when a task is due. This system ensures that nothing slips through the cracks.

Time management and productivity are skills that anyone can develop with practice. By implementing the techniques and strategies outlined in this chapter, you can take control of your time, accomplish more, and feel less stressed. Whether you use the Pomodoro Technique, the Eisenhower Matrix, or time blocking, the key is to find a system that works for you and stick to it. Remember, managing your time effectively isn't about being perfect—it's about making steady progress and working toward your goals in a balanced, manageable way.

Take control of your time, and your productivity will follow!

Chapter 8

Communication Skills for Remote Work

Remote work has transformed the way professionals interact and collaborate. Without the convenience of face-to-face meetings or casual office conversations, effective communication becomes the backbone of success in a remote work environment. In this chapter, we will explore key communication skills that are essential for remote work, discuss common challenges, and provide practical examples to help you navigate this new landscape.

Why Communication Skills Are Crucial for Remote Work

Remote work is built on trust, collaboration, and efficiency—all of which rely on good communication. Since remote workers are often spread across different time zones, regions, or even countries, clear and effective communication becomes even more important to ensure that teams are on the same page. The absence of in-person cues, such as body language or tone of voice, can easily lead to misunderstandings. Thus, remote workers need to develop strong written and verbal communication skills to bridge the gap created by distance.

Challenges in Remote Communication

Remote work presents specific communication challenges that are unique to this setup:

1. Lack of Non-Verbal Cues: In face-to-face communication, body language, facial expressions, and tone of voice play a huge

role in conveying meaning. In a remote environment, especially when relying on text-based communication, these cues are absent, which can lead to misinterpretation.

2. Time Zone Differences: Working across different time zones means that synchronous communication (e.g., phone calls or video meetings) may not always be feasible, leading to delays in responses.

3. Over-reliance on Text-Based Communication: Remote work often depends on emails, messaging apps, and project management tools, where tone and intent can be misunderstood.

4. Distractions and Multitasking: In a remote setting, distractions at home or outside the office may reduce the quality of attention, making communication less effective.

Key Communication Skills for Remote Workers

1. Clarity in Written Communication

Clear and concise written communication is the most important skill for remote workers. Whether through emails, instant messaging, or project management platforms, written communication is the foundation of remote work.

- Be Concise: Stick to the main points. Long-winded messages may lose the reader's attention or create confusion.

- Use Structure: Organize your messages clearly by breaking them into paragraphs, bullet points, or numbered lists. This makes your content easier to digest.

- Provide Context: Since your recipient may not have all the information readily available, give them the background they need to understand your message.

Example:

Instead of writing:

"Can you send the files I need for the project? I'm waiting to complete my task."

Write:

"Hi Maria, could you please send the final draft of the design files for the ABC project? I need them to complete my portion by the end of the day. Thank you!"

This message is more specific, includes context, and explains the urgency.

2. Active Listening in Virtual Meetings

Active listening is as important in virtual meetings as in in-person conversations. When you're working remotely, listening attentively during video or phone calls ensures that you understand the message and can respond appropriately.

- Avoid Multitasking: During virtual meetings, give your full attention to the conversation. Multitasking can lead to missing important details.

- Take Notes: Jot down key points from meetings to ensure that you retain important information and can refer back to it later.

- Ask Clarifying Questions: If something is unclear, ask questions to ensure you fully understand what's being communicated.

Example:

In a team meeting where the project timeline is being discussed, instead of simply nodding, you could actively participate by saying:

"Just to clarify, are we moving the deadline to Friday for the client review, or is that just for the internal team?"

This shows that you are paying attention and care about getting the details right.

3. Using the Right Communication Tools

Remote work offers various communication tools, each suited for different types of interactions. Knowing when to use each tool is key to effective communication.

- Emails: Best for formal communication, detailed explanations, or when you need to share documents. Emails are ideal for non-urgent matters that don't require an immediate response.

- Instant Messaging (e.g., Slack, Microsoft Teams): Great for quick questions, updates, or informal chats. However, avoid overloading team members with excessive messages, especially outside working hours.

- Video Calls (e.g., Zoom, Google Meet): Use video calls for more in-depth discussions, team meetings, brainstorming sessions, or when sensitive topics need to be addressed.

- Project Management Tools (e.g., Asana, Trello, ClickUp): Use these tools to track tasks, deadlines, and progress, ensuring that everyone stays on the same page.

Example:

If you need a quick confirmation on a task, sending a message on Slack like:

"Hey John, can you confirm if the report is ready for review?"

is better than writing a formal email for something that doesn't need much explanation.

4. Emotional Intelligence in Remote Work

Emotional intelligence (EQ) is critical in remote work since you're missing out on the physical office atmosphere. EQ involves being aware of your own emotions, as well as recognizing and appropriately responding to the emotions of others.

- Show Empathy: Be mindful of your colleagues' workload, time zones, or any personal challenges they may be facing in the remote work environment.

- Be Patient: Not everyone will respond immediately, especially if they are in a different time zone. Patience is key to maintaining positive relationships in a virtual work setting.

- Use Positive Language: Since tone can be hard to interpret in text-based communication, make an effort to use polite, positive language to avoid coming across as harsh or demanding.

Example:

Imagine you're following up on a task that's overdue. Instead of saying:

"Why haven't you finished this yet?"

Try:

"Hi Sarah, I hope you're doing well. Just checking in to see if you need any support to finalize the report. Let me know how I can help!"

This approach is empathetic and non-confrontational, making it more likely to get a positive response.

5. Setting Boundaries and Expectations

Remote workers often juggle different responsibilities and may work flexible hours. Clear communication about availability and expectations can prevent miscommunication and frustration.

- Set Availability Hours: Let your team know when you will be available for meetings or collaboration. Use calendar tools to block off time zones or working hours.

- Define Response Times: If you're unable to respond immediately, communicate your expected response time. This helps manage expectations and reduces pressure.

- Communicate Deadlines Clearly: Specify deadlines and timeframes for each task, making sure that all parties are aware of expectations.

Example:

In a message:

"I will be available from 10 AM to 4 PM EST today. If you need anything urgently outside of these hours, please feel free to leave a message, and I'll get back to you first thing in the morning."

This sets clear boundaries while ensuring your team knows when they can expect a response.

6. Adaptability and Flexibility

Remote work environments are dynamic, and things can change quickly. Being adaptable in your communication style will help you navigate these changes with ease.

- Be Open to Feedback: Whether it's about your work, communication style, or collaboration tools, welcome feedback from your team and make adjustments accordingly.

- Adjust Communication Style: Not everyone prefers the same mode of communication. Some may prefer detailed emails, while others may thrive in quick chat messages. Adapt your style based on the preferences of your colleagues.

Example:

If your manager prefers detailed updates via email instead of instant messaging, adjust your approach accordingly.

"Hi Michael, as requested, here's a summary of the project status with timelines for each task. Let me know if you need further details."

Being flexible with communication preferences builds stronger working relationships.

Mastering communication skills in a remote work setting can be challenging, but it is critical for your success. By focusing on clarity, active listening, emotional intelligence, and using the right tools for each interaction, you can build effective, productive working relationships with your remote colleagues.

Chapter 9

Financial Management for Freelancers

Freelancing can be an exciting and rewarding career path, offering flexibility and independence. However, it also comes with the responsibility of managing your own finances. Unlike traditional employees who rely on employers to handle things like taxes, retirement savings, and benefits, freelancers must do this themselves. In this chapter, we'll explore practical steps to master financial management as a freelancer, covering essential topics like budgeting, taxes, saving for retirement, and managing cash flow, all presented in simple, actionable ways.

1. Understanding Your Income and Expenses

The first step to managing your finances as a freelancer is getting a clear picture of your income and expenses. Unlike salaried employees, freelancers often face fluctuating income. Some months, you may land multiple clients or big projects, while other months may be lean. To get started, follow these steps:

Track Your Income

It's crucial to track how much you're earning each month. Use tools like spreadsheets, accounting software (e.g., QuickBooks, FreshBooks), or apps to keep track of your income from different clients.

Example:

Let's say in January, you earn $2,000 from Client A, $1,500 from Client B, and $500 from one-off projects. Your total income for January is $4,000. Track this carefully, as it helps you plan for both busy and slow months.

Track Your Expenses

Freelancers also have business-related expenses. These might include software subscriptions, equipment, marketing, travel, or even coworking space fees. Knowing how much you spend is crucial for budgeting and tax deductions.

Example:

If you spend $50 on software, $100 on internet, and $150 on office supplies, your business expenses for the month amount to $300. By tracking both income and expenses, you know that your profit (before taxes) for the month is $4,000 - $300 = $3,700.

2. Creating a Budget

Budgeting is crucial for freelancers to ensure that your income covers both business and personal expenses. Start by dividing your budget into two categories: personal and business.

Personal Budget

Your personal budget should include rent, utilities, groceries, health insurance, and entertainment. Since your income may vary month-to-month, calculate your average monthly personal expenses and aim to save enough during busy months to cover lean periods.

Example:

If your personal expenses average $2,500 per month, and in January you earn $4,000, try to save any surplus ($4,000 - $2,500 = $1,500) for future months when your income might be lower.

Business Budget

Create a business budget to cover essential operating costs like software, equipment, marketing, and other business-related expenses.

Example:

If you need to upgrade your laptop for $1,200 but don't have the funds immediately, plan to save over several months, setting aside $300 a month from your earnings.

3. Setting Aside Money for Taxes

One of the biggest mistakes freelancers make is forgetting about taxes. Since you don't have an employer withholding taxes from your paycheck, it's up to you to set aside money for tax payments.

Estimate Your Taxes

In most countries, freelancers must pay income tax, self-employment tax, and possibly local taxes. As a rule of thumb, set aside around 25-30% of your income for taxes. Use online tax calculators or work with an accountant to get an accurate estimate.

Example:

If you earn $4,000 in January, you should set aside at least $1,000 ($4,000 25%) for taxes. That way, you won't be caught off guard when tax season comes.

Paying Quarterly Taxes

In many places, freelancers must pay estimated taxes quarterly. Missing these payments can result in penalties. Keep track of deadlines and make sure to set aside money to make those payments on time.

Example:

In the U.S., estimated quarterly tax deadlines are typically in April, June, September, and January of the following year. If you expect to owe $12,000 in taxes for the year, plan to pay $3,000 each quarter.

4. Managing Cash Flow

Freelancers often face unpredictable cash flow. Some clients pay late, and projects can get delayed. It's crucial to manage your cash flow so that these fluctuations don't put you in financial stress.

Build an Emergency Fund

An emergency fund can help you get through lean months. Ideally, aim to save 3-6 months' worth of living expenses. This fund should be easily accessible (in a savings account) but separate from your daily business account.

Example:

If your monthly expenses are $3,000, aim to save at least $9,000 to $18,000 in an emergency fund. This will provide a buffer during slow periods or unexpected situations, like a medical emergency or a major client leaving.

Invoice Promptly and Follow Up

Ensure steady cash flow by invoicing promptly after completing work. Set clear payment terms (e.g., "net 30" means the client must pay within 30 days). Follow up if a client is late, and don't hesitate to send reminders or charge late fees if needed.

Example:

You complete a project for $1,000 on March 1st with a "net 30" payment term. You should send the invoice immediately, stating that payment is due by March 31st. If they don't pay by April 1st, follow up with a polite reminder.

5. Saving for Retirement

Freelancers don't have access to employer-sponsored retirement plans like 401(k)s, so you must take charge of saving for retirement on your own.

Open a Retirement Account

In many countries, there are retirement savings accounts designed for freelancers or self-employed individuals. In the U.S., you can open an Individual Retirement Account (IRA) or a Solo 401(k). These accounts offer tax benefits and help grow your retirement savings over time.

Example:

Let's say you contribute $500 a month to an IRA that earns 7% interest annually. Over 30 years, that $500 monthly contribution could grow into a retirement fund of over $600,000, thanks to compound interest.

Automate Your Savings

Consider setting up automatic transfers to your retirement account to ensure consistent contributions. Even if your income varies, try to save something each month. Aim to save at least 10-15% of your income for retirement.

Example:

If you earn $4,000 in January, contribute $400 (10%) to your retirement account. Even if February's income is lower, aim to contribute what you can, whether it's $100 or $300. Consistency matters over time.

6. Health Insurance and Other Benefits

Freelancers don't have employer-sponsored health insurance or benefits, so you'll need to purchase your own.

Health Insurance

Look for individual health insurance plans that fit your budget. You may also qualify for government subsidies or marketplace plans depending on your income. It's important to shop around and choose a plan that offers good coverage at an affordable cost.

Example:

If you find a health insurance plan that costs $300 per month, factor this into your personal budget to ensure that you're able to afford it without strain on your finances.

Other Benefits: Disability and Life Insurance

Freelancers should also consider disability insurance to cover your income if you're unable to work due to illness or injury. Additionally, life insurance can provide financial security for your family in case something happens to you.

Example:

Disability insurance could cost around $50 per month, and life insurance varies depending on age and coverage amount. Budget for these benefits to protect your income and loved ones.

7. Hiring Help

As your freelance business grows, you might find that managing finances becomes too time-consuming. In that case, consider hiring help.

Accountant or Bookkeeper

An accountant or bookkeeper can help you manage your finances, file taxes, and ensure you're taking full advantage of deductions. This can save you both time and money in the long run.

Example:

Let's say you pay a bookkeeper $150 a month. While this is an extra cost, it frees up your time to focus on high-value tasks, and it ensures your finances are organized and compliant with tax laws.

Financial Planner

A financial planner can help you create a long-term strategy for managing your income, taxes, retirement savings, and investments. This is especially useful if you're earning a substantial income and want to make the most of it.

Example:

If you hire a financial planner for $500 per year, they may help you discover better ways to invest or manage your money, potentially saving or earning you much more than their fee.

⎯⎯◉⎯⎯

MANAGING YOUR FINANCES as a freelancer can be challenging, but with the right strategies, you can take control of your money and build a secure financial future. Start by understanding your income and expenses, create a budget, set aside money for taxes, manage cash flow, and save for retirement. Remember to look after your health insurance and consider hiring professional help if needed. By applying these simple steps, you'll reduce financial stress and allow yourself to focus on growing your freelance career.

Chapter 10

Legal Considerations

When starting or running a business, understanding the legal landscape is essential. Legal considerations affect nearly every aspect of a business, from how it is formed to how it operates and interacts with customers, employees, and other businesses. This chapter covers some of the most critical legal concerns you need to be aware of, with real-world examples to help illustrate the key points.

1. Business Structure and Legal Entities

One of the first legal decisions you'll make when starting a business is choosing its structure. The legal structure you choose has significant implications for taxes, liability, and the day-to-day operations of your business. The most common business structures include:

- Sole Proprietorship: A business owned and run by one person. The owner is personally responsible for all the business's debts and obligations.

- Partnership: A business owned by two or more people. There are different types of partnerships, such as general partnerships, limited partnerships, and limited liability partnerships.

- Limited Liability Company (LLC): A flexible business structure that provides limited liability protection to the owners, meaning their personal assets are generally protected from business debts.

- Corporation: A more complex structure where the business is a separate legal entity from its owners, providing the highest level of liability protection.

Example:

Jane wants to open a coffee shop. She chooses to operate as a sole proprietor because it's easy to set up. However, after some time, she realizes that she could be personally liable for any debts or lawsuits related to the business. To protect her personal assets, Jane decides to convert her coffee shop into an LLC, which shields her personal wealth from business-related lawsuits and debts.

2. Intellectual Property (IP) Rights

Your intellectual property (IP) is one of your most valuable business assets. Intellectual property includes things like your logo, brand name, product designs, and any proprietary processes or inventions your business develops. Protecting your IP ensures that others can't steal or misuse your ideas.

There are several types of intellectual property protections:

- Trademarks: Protect words, symbols, logos, or designs that distinguish your brand from others.

- Copyrights: Protect creative works like books, music, films, and software from being copied or distributed without permission.

- Patents: Protect inventions, providing exclusive rights to make, use, or sell the invention for a certain period.

Example:

A company called "Bright Ideas" creates a new type of energy-efficient light bulb. To protect their innovation, they apply for a patent, which prevents competitors from copying their invention for 20 years. They also trademark their logo and brand name to ensure that no one else can sell similar products under the "Bright Ideas" name.

3. Contracts and Agreements

Contracts are legally binding agreements between two or more parties. They are essential for protecting your business when working with customers, suppliers, or partners. Well-written contracts can prevent disputes and misunderstandings by clearly outlining the responsibilities and obligations of each party.

Key elements of a contract include:

- Offer and acceptance: One party offers a service or product, and the other accepts.

- Consideration: Each party must exchange something of value, such as money, services, or goods.

- Mutual agreement: Both parties must agree to the terms of the contract.

Having a lawyer draft or review your contracts ensures that they are legally enforceable and protect your interests.

Example:

Sam's business, a catering company, enters into a contract with a local event venue to provide catering services for a wedding. The contract specifies the number of guests, the menu, the date of the event, and the payment terms. By having a signed contract, both Sam and the venue are protected in case of any disagreements. If the venue cancels at the last minute, the contract allows Sam to pursue legal action for the lost business.

4. Employment Law

If you hire employees, you need to comply with employment laws, which cover various aspects such as wages, working hours, discrimination, and workplace safety. Employment laws vary by country and region, but some key areas to be aware of include:

- Hiring and firing: Employment contracts should outline the terms of employment, including compensation, benefits, and termination conditions.

- Discrimination: It is illegal to discriminate against employees based on characteristics such as race, gender, age, religion, or disability.

- Workplace safety: Employers are responsible for maintaining a safe working environment for their employees.

Example:

Julia owns a small retail store. She hires two employees and ensures that they sign employment contracts that outline their job roles, working hours, and salary. Julia also attends a workshop on workplace safety to make sure she is providing a safe working environment. She installs non-slip mats in the stockroom and trains her employees on how to safely lift heavy boxes.

5. Data Privacy and Security

In today's digital age, businesses collect and store vast amounts of customer data, such as names, addresses, payment information, and purchase history. Data privacy laws regulate how businesses handle this sensitive information to protect consumers from identity theft and other cybercrimes.

Depending on where your business operates, you may be subject to regulations like:

- General Data Protection Regulation (GDPR): A European Union regulation that requires businesses to protect the personal data and privacy of EU citizens.

- California Consumer Privacy Act (CCPA): A state law that gives California residents more control over their personal information.

Ensuring compliance with data privacy laws involves implementing measures like secure data storage, encryption, and providing customers with clear privacy policies.

Example:

Tech startup Appify develops an app that collects user data to personalize their experience. Since Appify operates in Europe, they are required to comply with the GDPR. To do so, they update their privacy policy, get explicit consent from users before collecting data, and implement encryption to protect stored data. Appify also gives users the option to delete their data from the system.

6. Consumer Protection Laws

Consumer protection laws are designed to safeguard the rights of consumers and ensure fair trade practices. These laws regulate advertising, product safety, and customer service, among other things. Businesses must be transparent about their products and services, provide accurate information, and resolve customer complaints fairly.

Examples of consumer protection regulations include:

- Truth in Advertising Laws: Prohibit businesses from making false or misleading claims about their products.

- Product Liability Laws: Hold businesses accountable for any harm caused by defective or unsafe products.

Example:

A company that sells skincare products claims that its moisturizer can eliminate wrinkles in just three days. A consumer buys the product, but it doesn't deliver the promised results. The consumer can file a complaint under truth-in-advertising laws, which could lead to fines for the company and force them to change their advertising practices.

7. Licensing and Permits

Most businesses require some form of license or permit to operate legally. The specific licenses or permits you need depend on your industry and location. Common examples include:

- Business license: Grants you

permission to operate in a specific area. Most cities or counties require a general business license to legally conduct business.

- Health permits: Required for businesses that serve food or beverages, such as restaurants or food trucks. These permits ensure that the business complies with local health and safety regulations.

- Zoning permits: Ensure that your business operates in an area designated for commercial use. This is especially important for businesses run out of your home or industrial operations that may have noise, traffic, or environmental impacts.

Example:

Sarah wants to open a bakery in her neighborhood. Before she can start selling cupcakes, she needs to apply for a business license from the city. Since she will be serving food, Sarah also needs to obtain a health permit after passing a health inspection. Additionally, Sarah checks with the city's zoning office to confirm that her bakery complies with local zoning regulations for retail businesses.

8. Tax Obligations

Complying with tax laws is a critical legal responsibility for any business. Depending on your business structure, you may be required to pay different types of taxes, including:

- Income tax: Businesses must pay taxes on their earnings. Sole proprietorships, partnerships, and LLCs typically pay taxes through the owner's personal tax returns, while corporations are taxed separately.

- Sales tax: If you sell goods or services, you may need to collect and remit sales tax to the state or local government. Sales tax rates and regulations vary by jurisdiction.

- Payroll tax: If you have employees, you are required to withhold federal, state, and local taxes from their wages, including Social Security and Medicare taxes.

Example:

David owns a small e-commerce business selling handmade furniture. He operates as an LLC, so he pays income tax through his personal tax return. David also collects sales tax from customers who live in the same state where his business is based. Each month, he files a sales tax return with the state and remits the taxes he collected. When he hires his first employee, David sets up payroll to automatically deduct and pay the required payroll taxes to the government.

9. Legal Disputes and Litigation

Despite your best efforts, legal disputes can arise in business. These disputes may involve customers, employees, competitors, or business partners. Common types of disputes include:

- Breach of contract: Occurs when one party fails to fulfill its obligations under a contract.

- Employment disputes: Arise when employees feel they have been treated unfairly, such as being wrongfully terminated or experiencing workplace discrimination.

- Intellectual property infringement: Occurs when someone uses your intellectual property without permission.

In the event of a dispute, it's essential to have proper documentation and legal representation. Many businesses opt for mediation or arbitration to resolve disputes outside of court, as litigation can be expensive and time-consuming.

Example:

A software company hires a developer to create a custom app. The developer delivers the app late and fails to include all the promised features. The company sues for breach of contract, seeking compensation for lost business due to the delay. To avoid an expensive court battle, the company and the developer agree to resolve the dispute through mediation, where a neutral third party helps them reach a mutually acceptable solution.

10. Compliance with Industry-Specific Regulations

Many industries have specific regulations that businesses must comply with. For example:

- Healthcare: Must comply with the Health Insurance Portability and Accountability Act (HIPAA) to protect patient information.

- Finance: Financial institutions must follow regulations like the Dodd-Frank Act, which governs transparency and accountability in the banking industry.

- Environmental regulations: Manufacturing businesses may need to comply with environmental laws, such as the Clean Air Act or the Clean Water Act, which aim to reduce pollution and protect natural resources.

Understanding the regulations specific to your industry is crucial to avoid fines and legal penalties.

Example:

A chemical manufacturing company is subject to strict environmental regulations to prevent the release of harmful chemicals into the air or water. The company invests in proper waste disposal systems and regularly tests its emissions to ensure compliance with the Clean Air Act. Failure to follow these regulations could result in hefty fines and damage to the company's reputation.

<hr>

LEGAL CONSIDERATIONS are a crucial aspect of starting and running a business. From choosing the right business structure to protecting intellectual property, complying with employment laws, and handling disputes, understanding and addressing legal issues can help you avoid costly mistakes. As a business owner, it's essential to stay informed about the legal obligations that apply to your business and seek professional legal advice when necessary. Being proactive about legal matters not only protects your business but also helps build a foundation for long-term success.

Chapter 11

Continuous Learning and Growth

In today's fast-paced world, the ability to adapt and grow is more important than ever. Continuous learning is not just a personal choice; it's essential for professional success and personal fulfillment. In this chapter, we will explore the concept of continuous learning, its importance, strategies to implement it, and real-world examples of its impact.

What is Continuous Learning?

Continuous learning refers to the ongoing, voluntary, and self-motivated pursuit of knowledge for personal or professional development. It encompasses various activities, including formal education, online courses, workshops, reading, and experiential learning.

Why is Continuous Learning Important?

1. Adaptability: The only constant in life is change. Industries evolve, new technologies emerge, and job roles shift. Continuous learning helps individuals stay relevant and adaptable.

2. Career Advancement: Employers value employees who take initiative in their professional development. Continuous learners are often seen as more committed, engaged, and ready for new challenges.

3. Increased Knowledge and Skills: Learning new skills or deepening existing knowledge enhances confidence and

competence in one's role. This can lead to increased job satisfaction and performance.

4. Personal Growth: Learning doesn't just enhance professional skills; it also contributes to personal development. Engaging with new ideas and perspectives can lead to greater creativity, improved critical thinking, and a broader worldview.

Strategies for Continuous Learning

1. Set Learning Goals

Define clear, achievable learning goals to give your efforts direction. For instance, if you want to learn a new programming language, set a goal to complete an online course within three months. Breaking larger goals into smaller milestones can help keep you motivated.

Example: Sarah, a marketing professional, set a goal to improve her data analysis skills. She enrolled in an online course and aimed to complete one module each week.

2. Embrace Online Learning

The internet offers a wealth of resources for self-directed learning. Websites like Coursera, edX, and LinkedIn Learning provide access to courses on various subjects. These platforms often allow you to learn at your own pace.

Example: John, an engineer, took advantage of online platforms to learn about artificial intelligence. He completed a series of courses over several months and was able to apply his new skills in his job.

3. Join Professional Networks

Networking with peers in your field can lead to shared learning experiences. Attend workshops, webinars, or conferences to connect with others and gain insights from industry leaders.

Example: Lisa joined a local chapter of a professional organization related to her field. Through attending meetings and engaging with others, she learned about the latest trends and best practices, which helped her advance in her career.

4. Read Widely

Reading is a simple yet powerful way to expand your knowledge. Explore books, articles, and research papers in your area of interest. Diversifying your reading material can expose you to new ideas and concepts.

Example: Tom committed to reading one book per month related to his field. This practice not only improved his expertise but also sparked new ideas for his projects at work.

5. Seek Feedback

Regular feedback can help identify areas for improvement and inform your learning path. Constructive criticism from colleagues or mentors can provide valuable insights that guide your development.

Example: Emily asked her supervisor for feedback on her recent project. The constructive feedback she received helped her understand her strengths and areas for growth, leading her to seek training in project management.

6. Experiment and Reflect

Learning doesn't always come from formal education. Experimenting with new methods or ideas in your work can lead to valuable insights. Reflecting on these experiences can help solidify your learning.

Example: Mark tried a new approach to his sales strategy based on a workshop he attended. By reflecting on the results, he refined his approach and found greater success in closing deals.

Cultivating a Growth Mindset

A growth mindset is the belief that abilities and intelligence can be developed through dedication and hard work. This mindset is crucial for continuous learning as it encourages resilience and a willingness to embrace challenges.

How to Develop a Growth Mindset

1. Challenge Yourself: Step outside your comfort zone and take on new challenges. Embrace failures as learning opportunities.

2. Stay Curious: Ask questions and seek to understand the "why" behind concepts. Cultivating curiosity leads to deeper learning.

3. Celebrate Effort: Acknowledge the effort you put into learning, not just the outcome. This fosters a love for the process.

4. Surround Yourself with Growth-Oriented People: Engage with individuals who have a growth mindset. Their attitudes can inspire you to adopt similar behaviors.

Examples of Continuous Learning in Action

Example 1: A Professional Transition

When Alex decided to transition from teaching to instructional design, he knew he needed to enhance his skills. He enrolled in a certificate program for instructional design and took online courses in graphic design and e-learning tools. Through continuous learning, Alex successfully made the shift and found a rewarding job in a corporate training department.

Example 2: Adapting to Technology

Maria, a nurse, realized that telehealth was becoming increasingly important in her field. To adapt, she sought training in digital health technologies and attended webinars about best practices in virtual care. By embracing continuous learning,

Maria was able to enhance her skills and provide better care to her patients during the pandemic.

Example 3: Lifelong Personal Learning

James, a retired engineer, believes that learning should never stop. He spends his free time exploring new subjects, such as history and philosophy, through online courses and community college classes. This commitment to lifelong learning keeps him engaged and intellectually stimulated, allowing him to share insights with others and maintain a rich, fulfilling life.

Overcoming Barriers to Continuous Learning

While continuous learning offers numerous benefits, barriers can hinder the process. Here are some common challenges and strategies to overcome them:

1. Time Constraints

Many people struggle to find time for learning amid busy schedules. To tackle this, prioritize learning by setting aside dedicated time each week. Even 30 minutes a day can lead to significant progress over time.

2. Lack of Motivation

It's natural to feel unmotivated at times. To reignite your passion for learning, remember your goals and the benefits of acquiring new skills. Find topics that genuinely interest you, as passion fuels motivation.

3. Fear of Failure

Fear of making mistakes can be paralyzing. Embrace the idea that failure is a part of the learning process. Shift your focus from perfection to progress, and recognize that every mistake is an opportunity for growth.

Conclusion

Continuous learning is a vital component of personal and professional success. By adopting strategies that promote ongoing development and cultivating a growth mindset, individuals can adapt to changes, enhance their skills, and find greater fulfillment in their lives. Whether through formal education, online courses, or self-directed study, the journey of learning is one that should never end. Embrace the process, and let curiosity guide you toward a future filled with growth and discovery.

Chapter 12

Maintaining Work-Life Balance

In today's fast-paced world, maintaining a healthy work-life balance has become more important than ever. As work demands increase and personal lives become more complex, finding harmony between the two can feel like an uphill battle. In this chapter, we'll explore practical strategies for achieving a balanced life, illustrated with relatable examples.

Understanding Work-Life Balance

Work-life balance refers to the equilibrium between personal life and professional responsibilities. Achieving this balance is crucial for mental well-being, productivity, and overall happiness. Without it, stress levels can rise, leading to burnout, health issues, and strained relationships.

The Importance of Work-Life Balance

1. Mental Health: A balanced life reduces stress and anxiety, promoting better mental health.

2. Productivity: Employees with a healthy balance tend to be more focused and efficient.

3. Relationships: Spending quality time with family and friends strengthens personal bonds.

4. Personal Growth: Having time for hobbies and interests fosters personal development.

Signs of Imbalance

Before we dive into solutions, it's essential to recognize signs of imbalance:

- Constantly Tired: Feeling exhausted even after a full night's sleep.

- Neglected Relationships: Friends and family feel distant.

- Work Creep: Work hours invade personal time, such as checking emails late at night.

- Lack of Time for Hobbies: No time for activities you once enjoyed.

Example: Sarah's Struggle

Sarah, a marketing manager, often found herself working late to meet deadlines. She would skip family dinners and miss her kids' soccer games. Over time, she felt disconnected from her family and increasingly stressed. Recognizing these signs was her first step toward change.

Strategies for Achieving Work-Life Balance

1. Set Clear Boundaries

Establishing boundaries between work and personal life is critical. This might mean setting specific work hours and not checking emails outside of those times.

Example: John, an accountant, started turning off his work phone after 6 PM. He explained to his team that he would respond to emails the next day. This allowed him to enjoy evenings with his family without distractions.

2. Prioritize Tasks

Use techniques like the Eisenhower Matrix to categorize tasks by urgency and importance. This will help you focus on what truly matters.

Example: Emily, a project manager, began her week by listing her tasks. She identified urgent tasks and scheduled them first, leaving room for less pressing items later. This approach reduced her stress and made her feel accomplished.

3. Schedule Downtime

Just as you would schedule meetings, block out time for personal activities. This might include exercise, hobbies, or simply relaxation.

Example: Mark, a software engineer, began scheduling a weekly game night with friends. This simple act revitalized his social life and helped him recharge after a demanding week.

4. Communicate Openly

Talk to your employer and coworkers about your needs. Open communication can lead to flexible work arrangements or support from your team.

Example: Lisa, a teacher, discussed her workload with her principal. As a result, she was able to get assistance during peak times, allowing her more personal time.

5. Embrace Technology Wisely

While technology can help improve efficiency, it can also blur the lines between work and personal life. Use tools to help manage your time, but don't let them dictate your life.

Example: David, a freelancer, set specific hours for his work app notifications. Outside those hours, he enjoyed his time off without feeling the pressure of work emails.

Practice Self-Care

Self-care is vital for maintaining balance. This includes physical activities, mental relaxation, and time for reflection.

Physical Health

Engaging in regular physical activity helps reduce stress and improve overall health. Whether it's yoga, running, or simply taking a walk, find an activity that you enjoy.

Example: Clara started a morning jogging routine. This not only improved her fitness but also provided her with a peaceful start to her day.

Mental Well-Being

Meditation and mindfulness can significantly contribute to mental health. Even a few minutes of deep breathing can help center your thoughts.

Example: During lunch breaks, Sam began practicing mindfulness exercises. He found that these moments of calm helped him approach his work with a clearer mind.

Foster Supportive Relationships

Building and maintaining strong relationships with friends and family can provide a much-needed support network.

Example: Group Activities

Organizing regular get-togethers or activities with friends can strengthen relationships. It might be a monthly dinner, a book club, or even a weekend hiking trip.

Example: Tom and his friends set a monthly game night tradition. This not only strengthened their bonds but also gave them something to look forward to amidst their busy lives.

Flexibility is Key

In a world that often demands rigid schedules, flexibility is a game-changer. Finding ways to be adaptable can significantly impact your work-life balance.

Example: Anna's employer allowed her to work remotely on Fridays. This flexibility helped her manage errands and spend more time with her children, leading to greater satisfaction in both her personal and professional life.

Reflect and Adjust

Regularly evaluate your work-life balance. Life is dynamic, and what worked last month may not work now.

Example: After noticing increased work stress, Michael took a weekend retreat to assess his priorities. He returned with a clearer perspective and a revised schedule that better suited his needs.

Conclusion

Achieving a work-life balance is an ongoing process that requires intention and effort. By setting boundaries, prioritizing tasks, and fostering supportive relationships, you can create a fulfilling life that encompasses both professional and personal satisfaction. Remember, it's not just about managing time—it's about creating a lifestyle that nurtures your well-being.

By taking proactive steps and regularly assessing your needs, you'll find that maintaining balance is not only possible but also rewarding. Start today, and watch how these small changes can lead to significant improvements in your life.